Take Nothing for Your Journey

poems by

Michael E. Williams

Finishing Line Press
Georgetown, Kentucky

Take Nothing for Your Journey

Copyright © 2016 by Michael E. Williams
ISBN 978-1-63534-044-0 First Edition
All rights reserved under International and Pan-American Copyright Conventions.
No part of this book may be reproduced in any manner whatsoever without written permission from the publisher, except in the case of brief quotations embodied in critical articles and reviews.

ACKNOWLEDGMENTS

These poems first appeared in the following journals sometimes in different versions:
"A Mad King Weeps the Loss of His Son" *Southern Poetry Review.*
 "In the Library" *Illinois Quarterly*
"Night Vision" *Cold Mountain Review*
 "On A Sermon from I Chronicles" and "Entering the Seminary" *Anglican Theological Review*
"Take Nothing for Your Journey" and "Reminiscence" *Old Hickory Review*
"The Circuit Rider" *explor*
"Voices from Unseen Rooms" *Weavings: A Journal of the Christian Spiritual Life*
"Sarah's Bath" *The Spire*
"Storyway", "Professor Emeritus", and "The Quiltmaker" *Alive Now*
 "Song of the Shaman" first appeared in the anthology *Passage.*
"Wasp" and "On Center Hill" *Belle Rêve*
"Sarah Waking" and "Mud Pies" *Still: The Journal*
"The Snake Handler", "Black Snake", "Tubing White Oak Creek", and "Snipe Hunt" *The Pikeville Review*

Publisher: Leah Maines
Editor: Christen Kincaid
Cover Art: Susan Hay
Author Photo: Anne Broyles
Cover Design: Elizabeth Maines

Printed in the USA on acid-free paper.
Order online: www.finishinglinepress.com
also available on amazon.com

Author inquiries and mail orders:
Finishing Line Press
P. O. Box 1626
Georgetown, Kentucky 40324
U. S. A.

Table of Contents

Take Nothing for Your Journey 1
Reminiscence 2
Night Vision 3
In the Library 4
Entering the Seminary 5
On a Sermon Taken from I Chronicles 6
Song of the Shaman 7
Voices from Unseen Rooms 8
A Mad King Weeps the Loss of his Son 9
Sarah's Bath 10
Professor Emeritus 12
Storyway 13
The Quiltmaker 14
The Circuit Rider 15
How Do I Hold You 20
Wasp 21
On Center Hill 22
Sarah Waking 23
Mud Pies 24
The Snake Handler 25
Black Snake 26
Tubing White Oak Creek 27
Snipe Hunt 28
Art Project 29

for
Margaret
Sarah
and
Lizzy

Take Nothing for Your Journey
for Ernest Saunders

We went without weighing
what we gained by going.
We left the seasoned sanity
 learned in the academies,
and roamed with those who knew
but knew not how they knew.
We heard from them the tales and spells
spun at dusk on the back roads of the world.
We took darkness as our discipline,
gave our eyes to the earth for gems
and journeyed along other, more vivid, roads.
Our feet we left in the blood red clay,
our arms to oaks, our legs to the spring
leaping from beneath the limestone slab.
It received our bodies into its ancient sediments
like so many creatures now long extinct.
Our parting breaths were carried on the breezes.
We relinquished all but a few sad syllables
soaring like the raven's screams
down the hollow that lies between dusk and death.
Finally, only traces of our madness remained
glowing like foxfire on a cold Fall night.
The most precious gift is the last to go.

Reminiscence

We had not meant to grow old,
it's just that year to year
living together forever
at twenty was impossible.
When my hair fell out
I clowned with corn silk
pasting it to forehead
temple and crown. It peeped
like scarecrow's hair
from beneath a tattered hat.
When the dentist pulled
your last few teeth
we replaced them
with white shell pieces.
Each piece held a rainbow
trapped like an insect in amber.
We had not meant to go so far—
you, singing in whispers
the fragments of some remembered tune
through mother of pearl,
while the floor around my chair
is cluttered like a corn crib
after many shuckings.

Night Vision
    for Cormac McCarthy

Silently wise eyes cut the outer dark,
the tangled growth of night.
In fear we confer upon the owl wisdom,
And forget that he sees us in our darkness.

Lightning splinters fall like footsteps
across our long untended bottomland of sleep.
Our hearts are shaken by our own silences,
We are driven back into the houses of our births,
and rush to the window
only to see headlights devoured by darkness
on the mountainside above.

In the Library
    for Lucien Stryk

This is where your words come to sleep,
to rest from their busy-ness.
The nurse-smooth hands of student assistants
place each in its place, like children sleeping
between their parents at night.
They are nourished on fluorescent sun
and book dust in this green carpeted
boarding school.

        Perhaps someday
You will drive up to visit them
only to find that, like a jealous mother,
I have taken them to live at my house.

Entering the Seminary

It is this enigmatic quality of revelation
        that troubles us.
How next door in the garden Shakespeare's
        brass face stares
        mute and cold
        to some hidden purpose.
How the el grumbles into the night outside
        like the vindication
        of an angry god,
or perhaps in imitation of a vague threat
        of rain.

On a Sermon Taken from I Chronicles

    Jabez,
born in sorrow, lies in the ashes of his fear
like a letter half burned.

    honorable
he was, we are told, and blessed.

keep us from evil....
our prayers fall back into our throats
....that it may not grieve us
we have bitten our birthright into the quick
stalked the bright desert while praying for darkness
left our footprints on the moon
we have taken the bus tour of hell
guideless and alone
keep us....

    Jabez,
elder brother, we are told many things
on this shrunken coast of lies.

Song of the Shaman

When I was wizard of the daylight world
      I stalked the simpering deer
                              on foot.
Trees I metamorphosed into mountains.
                           Come see
my tricks
      come view
the vital juices dribbling in my stomach's cave.
I dressed in black
      to hide
        the glowing skin
                  from sun
      and brier
           and slept naked
in the needle flesh belly of earth.

I was court magician to the frozen lake
      I stopped the water's rush
                      like a photograph
remembered. Dusting with snow the crusted world
I sought the secrets of the fractured crystal.
                 The tree women
claimed my eyes were hazel
                  or green when the sun was bright.
Come let my snowdrift wand dazzle you.
                For when our eyes
are as dried as crushed leaves
                and the waters of the lake
              move once again,
      we shall walk along the shore in summer.
                I will sprinkle
sand over the water
            as green as wild onions
              and tell you
that I was wizard of the daylight world
and court magician to the north country
where the waters in winter
                thicken like blood.

Voices from Unseen Rooms

Faces from the past linger about the table
Hanging as still as the full moon
Against the dark sky of memory.
Sister, brother, parent, child
Singing in the blood, singing in the bone,
Remember me, remember me.

Voices call from unseen rooms
Echoing down the empty hall
Beckoning us to enter into
Worlds yet to be explored.
Sister , brother, parent, child,
Singing in the blood, singing in the bone,
Remember me, remember me.

On the breath of imagination
God speaks creation into place
In the midst of which another breathes
Dreaming of still other worlds.
Sister, brother, parent, child,
Singing in the blood, singing in the bone,
Remember me, remember me.

We taste the dust of mud bricks
On tongues that cannot forget,
And the bread of remembrance melts
Like a promise in the mouth.
Sister, brother, parent, child,
Singing in the blood, singing in the bone
Remember me, remember me.

Voices linger in the hollows of memory
Like the aroma of bread fresh from the stove
Enticing us back to feast on their sounds
And filling our hunger with the food of home.
Sister, brother, parent, child.
Singing in the blood, singing in the bone,
Remember me, remember me.

A Mad King Weeps the Loss of His Son

"....and if the moon should call you, my son,
Would you then turn your face toward home?"
Night whimpers in the windows,
The sullen brother wakes to tend
The animals, twice as many
As before. The servants wear their
Livery like a calm respect.
A sign, the light incessant burns.

The city sleeps. No one concerns
Himself to view the horrid aspect
Of clothes so sparse they seem to wear
The man. Thin and tinny
Voices of women sing the end
Of doom. None sings like the wind does.
"Would you then turn your face toward home
If the moon should call you, my son...."

Sarah's Bath

These are ancient waters
in which we play.
Once they spanned the banks
of sacred rivers;
Tigris, Ganges,
Niger, Euphrates.
We are pilgrims
come to wash away
that which we can
no longer name.

These are ancient paths
that brought us here.
the roads we share
with all who came before;
womb and water,
blood and waiting
are their names.
We come not knowing
our destination,
together stir the waters
for a time
and find in each other
home

These are ancient
languages
we speak
from a time when
the earth itself was
young;
dada, mama,
splash, wave,
gurgle, bye-bye.

We are the first speakers
once again
offering signs
across the waters
hoping to come through
pass over
join voices
across all that
divides us,
all that
binds us.

Professor Emeritus

My former teacher was a temperate man, a frequent
  guest speaker at the Rotary Club and
  departmental dinners, who neither ate
    nor drank nor talked too much
    and was loved for it.

In rented dining halls, where men in suits drew diagrams
  on paper napkins, he shared his anecdotes
  of Hawthorne, Whittier, and Frost.
    He never used a note
    and never failed to please.

Those who knew him as a young man say in those days
  he was given to extremes, speaking of conversations
  with imaginary companions
    or with animals,
    or relatives long dead.

Recently the failing of his youth returned. In public
  he asked the impertinent and completely
  unexpected question, "If I should fall
    in the forest alone,
    would the trees hear?

Now he sits in his rocking chair, a cat curled up
  in the crook of his arm, and hums a ballad
  that as a boy he'd heard his grandmother sing--
    or all that he remembers
    of it now.

Storyway

sing me a song
fresh from ancient lips
of the birth of the beautyway
sing me a song of new beginnings

tell me a story
older than the pollen and the sacred corn meal
from the time when people and creatures
taught each other
tell me a story
of the earth

remember me a tale
of the heroic dead in their seasons
who sang for their children and grandchildren
remember me a tale
to tell for others

remember me a tale
of the dancer and the dancer's grace
moved by the pain of the still heart
to record upon the wind
the people's last breath.

The Quiltmaker
for Mabell Futrell

The quiltmaker sits at her work
piecing from saved cloth
a cotton patchwork Book of Days.
It is her gift.

Her eye designs,
her hand displays
in gingham, domestic, and pastel
a kaleidoscopic star,
the little Dutch girl,
the double wedding ring
the drunkard's trail.
All are cut from the fabric of the past.
This, a scrap of her mother's dress,
that, the print from a flour sack,
the other, a piece never made up.
They are her gifts
which she gives away.

Sometimes her sister, my mother, pieces
while she unrolls the batting
and quilts a pattern of stitches
into this finished cloth of fragments.
The sisters speak of secrets shared in
  girlhood,
of movies my mother cried through,
which embarrassed her sister to death.
Now as my aunt prepares to join them
the names of the dead are invoked:
Neuma, Lela, Clara, Auntie, Dora,
teachers all, some quilters as well.

As dark settles in they sit and stitch
in a silence full of the past.
There are names for these stitches,
if only I could remember them now.

The Circuit Rider

I

After all the waves are waved
      the hands are clasped
           the blessing said
and proof of the appreciation
      made good,
big-bellied women, great with child,
      chase off to bed
           tow-headed boys.
Shuck stuffing sounds fall from
      youthful beds
           to slip like the outside night mist
                across the floor
                      unnoticed.
The wood inside fired bright
      to chase the evening chill
           from ancient bones
the grandfather stands outlined by the door-formed light,
      sees before his clouded eyes
           the union of the rider
                and the night.
The broad-shouldered black coat sits bowed
      against the angry angel of
           early springtime chill.
By the latch string the door is shut
      and light closed off, the dooryard is united
           with the rider and the night.

II

"Brother Night, the word spoken in the forest
        falls upon the stump seats in a hundred dooryards
in quieted tavern-stores and cellar-jails
        falls upon the stump-heads of hunters
the stump-ears of farmers,
        and like the hardened grease and gravy leavings
on the plate is thrown out
        left dripping off the porch in back.

This promised land once dreamt of
        now forces the dreamer back across the threshold
into darkness. This promised land
        now fertilized by immigrant bones and native blood
brings forth a thorny tree. This promised land
        now flows with milk and sour wine.
        Woe to them,
                the unfaithful,
soft beds support hard hearts.

What gain ye pioneer
        if ye gain the riches of a new-found world
                but lose thy immortal soul?
Woe to them that devise iniquity upon their beds
        the inheritors, now, dispossessed can only die.

III

           Night time.
The circuit rider passes
      unrestrained by light-colored day time,
unrequired in the cool evening time by anyone.
      The brother, night, slows down heated daytime thoughts
the night caresses day time stubbled cheek and chin.
      The rider moves like smoke—drifting suspended—
only to be blended into some rude moving breeze.
    Be still
The evening quiet leaves room and time enough
      for the unsaid words, the unthought thoughts the journey
long,
Antioch to Dickson. Only in the wilderness
      when night lies restless against the sky,
entwined by spindly fingered oaken guardians,
      can thoughts tied down by clearing, store, and cell,
Caught deep within the broadcloth covered belly, arise.
    And know
Desire like grief creeps up the rider's chest
      vested and coated against winter's rude
Intrusion into spring.
    Be still and know
The vineyard is darkened now,
      the yoke now set aside.
The ride is quiet. The rider braces against
      the visitation of the angry angel
of the night's mist and chill
      The words sleep, resting for the next day's labor.
The rider remains awake. Dark Solomon
      month-long bridegroom longing
leaves his ecclesiastic bride, metaphysical pleasure spent
      lies in the shuck bed half-sleep of the mind.
Only the dark angel, night, and rider remain awake.
    Solomon speaks
        How beautiful are thy feet

IV

"Soul keeper, work your magic
      though rough shod, covered poorly,
my own fair tower waits. It is late
      and two more days of riding left me."

The moonlight draws night madness
      from the rider's drumming veins
draws visions to the darkened forest.
      Cunning night brings forth the goblet and the jewels,
      displays before his seeking, sleepless eyes
            the pools of Heshbon.
The night angel only watching
      the rider climbs the spiced mountain.
            How beautiful are thy feet with shoes, pioneer daughter
The gingham covered tower, ivory in the rider's mind,
      not conjured by the stone-covered vintage of the muscadine
nor the hot corn essence cut with water from the creek.
      The night scent thickens, and so the blood
grows hot like summer noontime.
      How beautiful are thy feet

V

The dark watcher, wings folded, stands
	in the shadow of the Cumberland moon;
Solomon on his mountain.

How Do I Hold You?
for Lizzy

How do I hold you
my daughter, my wren
tall enough now to look me in the eye,
flinging words that fly my way
like water beads from wry wings?

How do I hold you
my dove, my fear
of the hunter palpable in my mind,
my mouth--like blood packed wounds
where wisdom teeth once were?

How do I hold you
my heron, sweet fisher
whom grief drives into depths
past all wonder?

When in your flight
you seek rest,
and your feet gain no purchase
on this not-so-solid earth
I will be waiting, keeping vigil.

Alight--abide a while.

Wasp

hydrangeas in a ball mason jar
a vine wreath encircling them
on a table made of weathered wood
the smell of sausage frying in a black skillet
sneaks through the open kitchen door
the wasp I failed to kill creeps back
and forth along the table's edge
he and I are cautious of each other now
we who are partners in hunger and death

On Center Hill

behind the scrim
of mist this
morning
the lake disappears
past the trees
past the porch
past the door

soon I will gather
kindling for tonight's
fire whose
light will
rival the fiery stars
rival the sun
that burns away
the scrim of
morning

beneath the porch
carved in relief
on a single log
an owl keeps watch
keeps her own counsel
keeps her wisdom
to herself

Sarah Waking

Your cry rips the darkness
yanks me up out of sleep
a swimmer forced to the
surface against his will.

I rise, navigate the autumn
darkened morning, and lift you from your
sleep world of bears and lambs
of dreams and flannel coverlets.

Together we dance our rocking dance;
you cannot tell me if or where it hurts.
Nor can I tell you of all that I would
keep you from, if only such keeping
were possible.

I stand at your window, listen
to rain on the leaves, watch the cold
gray light, the coming of winter.

Mud Pies

The rain overflowed
the half-clogged gutter
mingled with dirt making
puddles the color of coffee
softened with evaporated milk
we pilfered my mother's pans
barreled through the sopping yard
to shove our hands
into the brown pudding
of the first and last
ingredient of our lives.

The Snake Handler

Work callused hands hold the leash
of whatever is beyond, arm trembling
 in a scaly handshake this preacher
and his snake sway in faith's dark dance.

Serpent,
you who lived that we might die,
that we might know death and know it abundantly.
When life is spent in worry and waste
by those who work and weep and lie
asleep in their ticking plots,
is it you they see?

He speaks in tongues released
from the common languages of earth,
and trusts beyond the yielding serpent's touch,
believing he will live while those of lesser faith
perish. Doubter that I am, I ask,

Will death spare such
as these and in his kingdom
keep them whole?

Black Snake

A black snake slipped between thick stems of grass
let go to seed. My dad said we'd have to take the blade to it.
We had not, though, and the snake made its home
between the outhouse and the packed dirt edges of the yard.

I saw the flexing black tube of its body pass
between my feet and the tall, wild grass.
Fearful of this creature that meant me no harm
I rushed to grab the hoe and kill it.

When I returned the snake has escaped. I placed the hoe
back on its hook and since that day have wondered,
what dark and friendly presence will I attempt
to do away with next?

Tubing White Oak Creek

we drop the tubes at brown's camp
past the spring that feeds the creek

in the chilling flow of white oak
we shudder until our bodies cool

the creek is up past the bridge at Magnolia
up past those fishing shirtless, careless

one shouts, *them's the whitest laigs
I ever seen.* then, *wont some tea?*

I decline but he insists, so I taste the tea
from the red plastic cup against my friends' advice

the sweetness is an icy fire in my mouth.
I taste the cigarette smoke infused into its amber

I wave goodbye as my tube slides as easily
as time beneath magnolia bridge

believing that I'm
the one that got away

Snipe Hunt

Snipe priests on the cusp of adolescence,
we come to these rites carrying burlap sacks.
 "You'll hear them," we say.
"Trap them in the bag," we tell them.
Then we abandon our initiates to their vigil
among the shadow-painted trees.
We leave them to their lives that pass as swiftly
as the breeze sneaking through the dark wood
to billow their empty sacks until there is
no light left by which to see.

Art Project
    for Lizzy

one ceramic shoe
glazed bronze
like a baby shoe
one that knew
the ecstasy of feet
running or walking
the artist's hand
in covenant with clay
captures one
worn shoe

the weariness of sneakers
the lethargy of laces
the solitude of soles

in the proper light
an iridescence gazes
out like an exile who can't
quite bring to mind a single
memory of her former life
nor that ancient tale
that bears repeating
if only the words
would come

Michael E. Williams was born in Murray, Kentucky and has spent most of his life in Tennessee. He was educated at Vanderbilt University, Garrett-Evangelical Theological Seminary, and holds a PhD from Northwestern University. Michael is a United Methodist pastor, who has lectured at Princeton Theological Seminary, Emmanuel College of The University of Toronto, Morehead State University, and at a number of other colleges and universities. He has been a featured teller at the National Storytelling Festival in Jonesborough, Tennessee, has taught workshops on writing and storytelling across the country and has been publishing for over four decades. He is the author or editor of twenty non-fiction books, and has written three plays that have been produced. His poetry has appeared in *The Southern Poetry Review, Appalachian Heritage, Southern Humanities Review, Cold Mountain Review, Still, The Pikeville Review,* and other journals. While he was a student a collection of his poems was awarded the Academy of American Poets Prize at Northwestern University. He lives in Nashville, Tennessee where he serves as Senior Pastor of West End United Methodist Church.

www.ingramcontent.com/pod-product-compliance
Lightning Source LLC
LaVergne TN
LVHW041509070426
835507LV00012B/1427